MW00387499

This book belongs to:

____